Digital Photography Inside Out!

DISCLAIMER AND TERMS OF USE AGREEMENT:

(Please Read This Before Using This Report)

This information in this course is for educational and informational purposes only. The content is not presented by a professional, and therefore the information in this course should not be considered a substitute for professional advice. Always seek the advice of someone qualified in this field for any questions you may have.

The author and publisher of this course and the accompanying materials have used their best efforts in preparing this course. The author and publisher make no representation or warranties with respect to the accuracy, applicability, fitness, or completeness of the contents of this course. The information contained in this course is strictly for educational purposes. Therefore, if you wish to apply ideas contained in this course, you are taking full responsibility for your actions.

The author and publisher disclaim any warranties (express or implied), merchantability, or fitness for any particular purpose. The author and publisher shall in no event be held liable to any party for any direct, indirect, punitive, special, incidental or other consequential damages arising directly or indirectly from any use of this material, which is provided "as is", and without warranties.

As always, the advice of a competent legal, tax, accounting, medical or other professional should be sought. The author and publisher do not warrant the performance, effectiveness or applicability of any sites listed or linked to in this course.

All links are for information purposes only and are not warranted for content, accuracy or any other implied or explicit purpose.

This report is © Copyrighted. No part of this may be copied, or changed in any format, or used in any way other than what is outlined within this course under any circumstances. Violators would be prosecuted severely.

Contents

- Digital Photography
- The Basics Of Digital Imaging
- Digital Imaging Software
- Tips for Taking Great Digital Photos
- Digital Scanning Basics
- Digital Photography Basics
- Digital Cameras and the Benefits
- Combination Digital Cameras—Not So New
- How to Buy Photography Equipments
- Black and White Photography
- A Career In Fashion Photography
- Food Photography Tips for Newbie's
- Proper Makeup As A Technique In Photography
- How To Capture Those Perfect Wedding Moments
- The Use Of Filters In Photography
- Focus And Get The Best Out Of A Shot
- Use A Telephoto Lens For Your Aquarium
- Techniques For Underwater Photography
- Forensic Photography Used In Today's Society
- Digital Stock Photography's Ability to Sell for You
- Should You Go to Photography School?
- Schools That Teach Photography
- How To Start A Photography Business

Digital Photography Inside Out!

Digital Photography

The constant and new advancements that are being found in digital photography have made it possible for your special moments to be captured with far better accuracy and detail than ever before. The new and improved photo resolution and shutter speed, help to make it easier for both professional and novice picture takers take excellent pictures. When these features don't help photos be materialized, advanced editing options that come with digital photography these days lets your pictures do full justice to the moments they capture.

Any photographer that is worth his salt will tell you that when 9it comes to taking good photos, timing is everything. There is a very small window of opportunity to capture a truly great shot, and whether you're after that sunset or trying to capture that all important race's winner, your fingers must have precision timing and an intuitive sense of when to snap. It's tougher than it looks, and it's why photography is really considered an art form.

Most of us only come close to getting the ideal shot and never quite realizing it in the end. More often than not, our pictures have most of the elements, but the also have a tendency to fall short in a few key areas. Perhaps you frame your subject well, but the lighting is just a little bit off. Or perhaps the lighting is good but you forgot to include a flash or to use red-eye reduction settings. This is where modern digital photography becomes a necessary component in getting the perfect look for your photo.

Within minutes, just about any picture can be edited to reach its full potential when it is created with a digital camera. Automatic color enhancement, red-eye reduction, and zoom and crop features that go along with taking digital photos are just a few of the many awesome features that digital photos have to offer. With these tools in easy reach, taking beautiful pictures becomes easier than ever.

Digital photography could be accomplished without a good digital camera as well as photo software. Your camera's ability is only the beginning. It is your vessel for taking the perfect picture, but from here it is up to your software programs to help you to truly make the most out of your pictures. This is where the magic happens. By magic, I mean that you can use your picture software to change your images and do whatever you want to.

Digital Photography Inside Out!

If you really want to be able to take excellent digital photographs, you can certainly find everything that you need including the camera and the software online or at your local retailers. Digital cameras are so popular these days you can find them just about anywhere. You just want to find a camera that will do what you want it to. You want a camera that offers great pictures as well as easy docking options for downloading to your printer or computer. You can edit your pictures as you like with programs like Kodak Picture, and Corel photo software.

Digital Photography Inside Out!

Digital Cameras

If you have ever wondered just what a digital camera does; how expensive it is; all of the features it has, or even how it got started all together, this is where you will get the information that you need about digital cameras. Digital cameras are the main component that you will need in order for you to be able to take digital photography to the next level. A good camera will certainly take all of the pain away from trying to capture the best picture possible.

Digital cameras basically look like your average 35mm cameras but they also look a bit like small video camcorders do. Instead of using film like the 35 mm cameras, they use a tiny light sensitive chip to capture an image. Because of this, these cameras can store from forty to eighty images inside its on-board memory. After shooting is finished, you attach the camera to a computer by way of a serial cable, and the imagery is copied right onto your hard drive.

As soon as technology becomes leaner and cheaper, digital cameras are gaining vast popularity among both the corporate sector and recreational users. Thanks to some of the brands and models that are featured today, the quality and reliability of digital photography continues to change the way we record a lifetime of memories. Though the images rendered lack a bit of the crispness of silver halide photographs (just as Polaroids seemed to flatten images out when they first came on the scene), the difference is rarely seen when it is placed on a computer screen, which is the great benefit of digital photography.

Digital cameras owe their existence to the NASA space program. The first interplanetary missions to Mars and the outer planets such as the *Viking Orbiter* and *Voyager* made use of variations on old television camera vacuum tubes known as vidicons. In 1969, a new development in image capture called Charge Coupled Device (CCD) technology caught the eye of NASA techs who immediately set about refining the size of the CCD pixel arrays. Hence, the digital camera got its beginning.

When you are ready to buy your digital camera, you need to take the price into consideration, but it is more important to think about the feature of the camera that you buy. It is the features that will help you to make the most of your pictures. You will not need a feature filled camera if you are only using it for recreational purposes. However if you plan to do a lot with your photos,

Digital Photography Inside Out!

you will want a camera that offers the right features for you. You can find a camera anywhere but you can t get some great deals online.

Digital Photography Inside Out!

Digital Imaging

Digital imaging has come a long way since those days when clunky digital cameras were those that were left in charge of the process a decade ago. The days are gone when you had to use the heavy, metal cameras that needed to be dragged from one event to the next. These days, digital cameras are smaller, lighter, and more compact than ever before. In fact, many of these tiny digital wonders can fit inside of your back pocket or purse.

Just so that you know, the huge selection of digital imaging equipment is both comforting and overwhelming when you have to begin choosing. There is little to no doubt that it makes it easy to ensure a good buy on a camera, but it also makes it difficult to choose which pieces are best for you and what your skill level is along with your needs. However, with just a bit of basic research done beforehand, it should be easy for you to evaluate the major contenders and to make an informed decision before buying.

Choosing Your Digital Imaging Equipment

When you are deciding on a digital camera to purchase, there are a few key considerations that you may want to take into account first. The first decision is in regards to your overall camera needs. You have to think of how often you will be using the camera and where you will be taking the majority of your pictures. Also, you need to think about how discriminating you are when it comes to things like picture composition and resolution.

After you've established your basic picture taking needs, you can turn to price and size considerations next, since you know that these will severely limit your options a bit it will be worth it. Many online retailers offer services that are geared toward helping their customers balance camera needs with camera costs properly. Finally, when you have narrowed the pool down to only a few key choices, you will want to think about finer details such as mega pixels and other camera features.

There are so many features that are out there that you can definitely find the perfect camera. Some come fully loaded with modern technology whereas others come with specific features. All you really need to do is asses your needs and desires, and if need be, get the help of a professional to choose the perfect bit of equipment for your digital imaging. It's that easy. My

Digital Photography Inside Out!

favorite place to find good equipment is Radio Shack or the Future Shop. Best Buy is pretty good when it comes to prices as well as Staples. You can search online, but at least with the retailers, you get professional assistance and a better return option if the equipment isn't quite up to par.

Digital Photography Inside Out!

The Basics Of Digital Imaging

In order for you to be able to get the most from your camera, it helps to know a few digital imaging basics. You don't need to be a pro or to enroll in photography classes to get yourself started. With just a bit of basic background information, it is easy to improve the quality of your work a great deal. This process starts by choosing good equipment. Imaging isn't very difficult once you get the hang of it. It's mostly in understanding the terms that are often used and then from there it's all gravy.

Learning About the Digital Method

When it comes to the many things that you have to consider, such as: the basic format of a digital photograph which is probably your most important aspect of it. How it works is that each image your camera captures is made up of tiny bits and pieces that are compressed together. Each image creates a bit-mapped graphic that is made up of pixels. If you are not clear on exactly what a pixel is you are not alone. The term "pixel" is nothing more than industry jargon for picture element, and, in a specific graphic, there are many, many square picture elements or pixels that come together to form the image as a whole.

Pixels are important in digital imaging because they are related directly to the quality of the group of images that they produce. Specifically, pixel size and depth will determine the space and color resolution respectively. Because of this, if you opt for a camera that make the most out of pixel performance you can usually improve the quality of the images you capture from the very beginning.

Professionals tend to have a more objective eye in this arena, which is what makes them more reliant on digital cameras with very high pixel counts. However, the average person can get by with much less. Thankfully, with growing market competition, there are a huge variety of digital cameras to consider in every price and feature range.

The cameras and software that you can get can be found anywhere on earth....literally. you can search online for good deals, but I would suggest that you go in store for your purchases and

Digital Photography Inside Out!

just use the internet to decide which cameras and software that you will use. My favorite place to find good equipment is Radio Shack or the Future Shop. Best Buy is pretty good when it comes to prices as well as Staples. You can search online, but at least with the retailers, you get professional assistance and a better return option if the equipment isn't quite up to what you would expect.

Digital Photography Inside Out!

Digital Imaging Software

Digital imaging software is a major aspect of digital photography. Without it, you just couldn't create or edit your digital photographs properly. This software has also evolved considerably in recent years. For example, most of the software is far more user friendly than its earlier versions, and this software is easy to install and operate. What then happens is that it has never been easier to create outstanding, high quality prints especially if you are a newbie.

The Technology of Digital Imaging Software

It used to be that digital imaging software was quite limited as to what it could actually do. You could upload prints from your camera to your computer and make a few minor adjustments and that seemed to be all. If you wanted to make dramatic changes like the pros do, however, you were out of luck. You were pretty much stuck with your original print as it was, flaws, red eye and all. Thankfully, those days are gone and new technology has opened the doors to a whole new world of opportunity when it comes to editing your pictures.

These days, there's nothing you can't do with good software and a decent camera. There are, of course, all of the basic features you might expect, including red eye reduction and zoom and crop features. However, that's really just the beginning of what digital software can do. Many programs offer automatic color correction and light enhancement to help you to make up for times when the flash didn't quite get the job done. Also, with new customization options, it is possible to imagine and create just about any edit you can imagine.

With all of this there is also the modern state-of-the-art editing options, most digital imaging software can be used to help you file, store, and organize your photos in original ways. These are handy, timesaving things that make it easy to save and share your favorite pictures with family and friends. If you're not using digital software, you should really take a moment to consider a few of the many ways that it might improve your photography experience.

If you are not sure about what type of software that you should be buying, you may want to chat with some friends who do or a find a good professional. They can help you realize exactly what software you need to do the job that you want it to. Some software will even send your pictures over email if you want it to. Take some time and search for your software before you buy and if

Digital Photography Inside Out!

you can get a review of it. You can find great reviews at www.cnet.com/reviews on all of your software needs.

Digital Photography Inside Out!

Tips for Taking Great Digital Photos

Digital photography is a new phase of technology that allows picture takers to experience instant gratification. When you do it properly, you can instantly get and edit your pictures to be as cool and interesting as you saw it in your mind when you were taking the pictures. Here are the steps that you can take to make the most out of all of your pictures.

Step One - If you have any experience with traditional 35mm photography, you will discover that there are some obvious and immediate differences when you start using your brand new digital camera. There are a few things to look out for and features that you will want to enjoy. What does this mean? Choose the right camera.

Digital Techniques: There are some professional and serious amateur photographers who will cringe at the thought of the low resolution photos that you get with a computer, because they feel that it ignores the actual art form that is called traditional photography. Don't get confused though because digital photography is here, it's big, and it's the way things are going to be from now on. Personally, I believe that traditional film photography will be a thing of the past within ten years other than those few die-hard fans of it who will likely refuse to give it up.

There are a lot of questions from the average people about what to look for when choosing a digital camera. For them I will guide you through flash and red eye filtering basics, the options that you will need to consider for transfer of digital data, and differences in zoom lenses.

Quick Fix: first of all, you will need to get rid of dust and specks, balance all of the colors, create a matte or mask, and then merge images. There's a lot you can do with modern photographic editors that we have these days. Here's a few tips that will help you make your picture perfect.

Creating Real time photos: Putting your photography into motion in 360° panorama has never been easier than it is right now. You can do a lot of things like picking a spot, to setting your camera for multiple frames, then stitching your shots together in movie format. Doing this will let you give your personal web site an interactive look and feel with this cool tool.

Digital Photography Inside Out!

3Digital Photo Storage: You may not think much of it when you're first starting out, but over a certain period of time, storing digital photographs on your computer can become a hard disk resource constraint. You also want to protect the readability of your electronic photo album.

Digital Photography Inside Out!

Digital Scanning Basics

Digital scanning is a new and very innovative extension of the technology that has provided us with first-rate digital cameras and imaging equipment for the past 10 years. These days, it is possible to scan just about any hard-copy document and to translate it into a digital format in only seconds. This allows each of us to accomplish easy editing, preservation, and dissemination of all of our important documents. In fact, a wide range of uses and a plethora of resources make it well worth considering the use of a digital scanner in your home or office.

The Many Uses of Digital Scanning

When most people think of digital scanning, they think of the average services that allow a hard-copy photograph to be scanned into digital format and posted in emails. This is especially helpful with old photos that may no longer have the negatives within easy reach. These photos can be stored digitally and can even be restored with modern editing and imaging software.

However, this is not the only use for digital scanning. Many colleges and school settings rely on scanning to upload key course materials to the Web page for them. Not to mention that with the proper copyright approval, selected course readings may be scanned and uploaded with the greatest of ease. This allows for easy access by students and for cheaper departmental material costs. The final result is that digital scanning is a widespread practice on most college campuses that we see today.

The possibilities truly are endless with digital scanning, making it well worth considering the purchase of a digital scanner. Prices for these have fallen considerably in recent years, as well which places these handy devices within reach of professionals and the rest of us alike. A quick look online or in the Sunday paper is likely to find you more than a few great deals.

Digital scanning just has become one of my favorite tools at my computer. If you are like me, chances are a good all-in-one device is going to save you much time and space. These devices do everything from scanning photos to sending faxes, printing and even act as a photocopier. The average home office would not be complete without one.

Digital Photography Inside Out!

Digital Photography Basics

There are so many advancements that are being found in digital photography that have created a better means of saving your memories. We now have new and improved photo resolution which really helps to make it easier for both pros and newbie's to take excellent pictures. Digital cameras are the probably the greatest thing to happen to photography since the original 35MM.

Any good photographer that is worth his salt will tell you that when it comes to taking good photos, timing is everything. There is a very small window of opportunity to capture a truly great shot, and whether you're after that sunset or trying to capture that all important race's winner, your fingers must have precision timing and an intuitive sense of when to snap. It's tougher than it looks, and it's why photography is really considered an art form.

Most of us only come close to getting the right picture and never actually get to the point where it follows completely through without blurs etc. you may be good at setting the frame, but the lighting is just a little bit off so your picture is crap. Or perhaps the lighting is good but you forgot to include a flash or to use red-eye reduction settings. This is where digital photography becomes a necessary component in getting the perfect look for your photo. Why not get into digital and get a better picture than with the rest.

Digital Photography Inside Out!

Digital Cameras and the Benefits

There are so many questions when it comes to digital photography such as; how expensive it is; all of the features it has and can perform, or even how it got started all in the taking over of photography. Digital cameras are the most important aspect of picture taking that you will need in order for you to be able to take digital photography to the next level. A good camera is the needed thing in order for you to be able to take all of the pain away from trying to capture the best picture that you can.

Digital cameras can't really be recognized by sight alone. They look a bit like small video camcorders do. Instead of using film like the other cameras do, they use a tiny light sensitive chip to capture an image instead. Because of this, these cameras can store a great deal more images than the others can and it is stored in the memory. After shooting is finished, you attach the camera to a computer by way of a serial cable, and the pictures go directly to the hard drive.

Digital cameras are a lot cheaper than they used to be now too because the technology is not so new anymore. Now that there are the many brands and models that are featured, the quality and reliability that comes with digital photography continues to change the way we keep track of moments. The difference is rarely unobserved.

Digital Photography Inside Out!

Combination Digital Cameras—Not So New

Digital cameras are starting to become less attractive than all in one digital camera which can often do many things other than just snapping photos such as record video, and play music. This is definitely the case with true in the Panasonic digital camera models. So that they could show this wonderful technology, this article will look at one of the combination digital cameras. One of these such cameras is the Panasonic SV-AS10 D

It is a combination of four devices in one: you get a 2 mega pixel digital camera, a camcorder, an MP3 player, and a voice recorder combined into one small device. This is one handy device to have around for anything that you may need done and to make things easier, the menu system is accessed by way of a small orange track ball that makes flipping between layouts easier than buying it.

Cameras like the all in one Panasonic camera is simply perfect for the gadget minded buyer and just about everyone else as well. It has designed image processing system delivers lush, and free images in resolutions of up to 1600x1200. what makes this so cool is that you can even watch movies and edit them too with QuickTime Pro and modified using Windows-compatible applications or converted to AVI files. That is simply cool. If you really want a fully featured digital camera, the combination cameras arte the way to go.

The Basics of Digital Imaging 1

Digital imaging is the reason that taking digital photos is so worth while. Without the right imagery taking digital photos wouldn't be worth the time. The days are gone when you had to use the heavy, metal cameras that needed to be dragged from one place to another. These days, digital cameras are smaller, lighter, and more compact than ever before. In fact, many of these tiny digital wonders can fit inside of your back pocket or purse with little to no effort at all.

Keeping in with this trend, the huge selection that we now of digital imaging equipment is both useful and practical when you have to begin choosing between them. There is no doubt that it makes it easier for you to get a good buy on your next digital camera however it also makes it extremely hard to choose which sections are best for you and what your skill level is along with your needs. You must learn however that if you take just a bit of time to do basic research

Digital Photography Inside Out!

ahead of time, it should be easy for you to evaluate the major contenders and to make an educated choice when you get to buying your camera.

When you are choosing a digital camera to purchase, there are a few major things that you need to think of. The first decision that you have to make is going to be based around your overall camera needs. You have to think of how often you will be using the camera and where you will be taking the majority of your pictures. Also, you need to think about how important composition and resolution really are to you. This is usually based on what you plan to do with your pictures once they are taken.

The Basics of Digital Imaging 2

If you want to be able to get the most from your camera, there are a few digital imaging basics. You don't need to be a professional photographer to get yourself started. With just a bit of basic background information, it is easy to improve the quality of your work a great deal. Doing this starts with getting the best equipment. Imaging isn't very difficult once you get the hang of it.

You will also want to think of things like: the basic format of a digital photograph which is very important. How it works is that each image your camera captures is made up of tiny bits and pieces that are compressed together or mega pixels. The term "pixel" is nothing more than another way to say picture element. All pictures have small elements that make the whole thing.

Pixels are important in digital imaging because they are directly in tune with the quality of the group of images that they produce. In general, pixel size and depth will help to decide the space and color resolution that you will be getting. Because of this, if you buy a camera that offers excellent pixel quantity, you are home free as to how your digital imaging goes. From there it is just editing.

Digital Photography Inside Out!

How to Buy Photography Equipments

Photography has been a popular hobby for over a hundred years now. Many get into this because it fascinates them, others just want to take the odd family picnic snapshots while yet others make it their means of living. But there is such a variety of equipment to choose from it can leave the mind boggling. Very often people go and buy the wrong thing, only to resell it at half the price after a few months. The most important accessory to your photography kit is the camera itself, and we will discuss buying a camera in this article.

Three tips on buying a camera

1. Get exactly what is required

Try and read yourself. Are you new to photography? What is the purpose of you buying a camera? Is it for snap shots? Or is it for professional work? A professional doesn't need this advice, but if you are a beginner do not buy the most expensive automated equipment even if you can afford it. Neither would you want a point and shoot model, which is only for the picnic people. You will want a camera with a few manual controls to help you learn about what changes in the settings can affect the final result.

2. Do your homework

If you are looking to buy a camera, try and get to know about some of the models on the market before you go to the dealer with your money. Read magazines, and websites to check out some of the latest reviews on the new models. Chances are they will help you get your hands on the one that is just right for you. Steve's Digicams is a website that has been reviewing cameras for quite a few years now, and whichever model you are looking at, old or new, chances are you will find a review here on Steve's. Once you read about what you want and check it out on the net, it will motivate you to read more about it, save the money to buy it, and buy the right one.

3. Stick to your budget

This is going to be hard, because the more you learn about photography the more sophisticated the camera model that you want. It is quite depressing when you know what you want and why you want it and cannot afford it. But did you know, some of the top photographers stick to the

Digital Photography Inside Out!

basics to get their images right? Agreed that it is cool to have the latest gadgetry on the market, but that is not what will impress on your folio. Make sure you have a good SLR camera and a good lens to back it up. Concentrate on the basics. Once you make a good folio, and if you become a successful professional, nothing can stop you from buying the best on the market.

Digital Photography Inside Out!

Black and White Photography

B & W photography was the first successful form of photography. It was popularized by Eastman Kodak in the first half of the previous century. It used simple silver halides as a coating on film. When light struck a part of this film, it burnt to black and where light did not fall on the film, it remained white. So blacks came out as white and vice versa, on the negatives. A reprint of the negative was in fact a positive, or the 'print'. This simple chemical process could be done at home by amateurs right from stage a to z.

The fall of B & W

There was nothing going the way of B & W once color hit the markets. All but a few enthusiasts switched to color. As far as people's mentality goes, a color TV is better than a black and white one, and the same applied to photographs. Once color film was introduced, black and white took the back seat. And once digital showed up, well that seemed like the last nail in the black and white coffin. Or did it?

The rise of B & W

In this modern day and age of digital cameras, scanners, desktop printers, super fast film and such, who would want to mess around in a black and white darkroom? Well, people who understand the rest of this article maybe. Did you know you could use color filters to create unique effects on black and white film? Yes! Try using a red filter and shoot an outdoor scene. the sky comes out almost black! Nothing else can give this effect. Photoshop ? No! Nothing can give quite the same effect as a color filter on black and white film. It is all about complimentary colors. Red, Blue and Green are primary colors that have opposites in the form of Cyan, Magenta and Yellow. As far the dark sky example goes - here is what happens. The Red filter lets all light rays pass through it to the film except for its opposite or complimentary color cyan, which is what the sky is mostly made up of. So, you get a dark sky. If you wanted to make grass appear dark what would you do? You would use a color filter of the color opposite to green, or complimentary to green, which is yellow. Every single blade of grass would turn darker, while the rest of the image looks fine. Can you imagine the possibilities with using color filters on black and white? You can MAKE your photographs exactly as you want them to be, and no two

Digital Photography Inside Out!

photographers need shoot the same scene to make it look all the same. This is the charm of B & W that no one will ever be able to take away, computer or no computer!

Digital Photography Inside Out!

A Career In Fashion Photography

We can get a glimpse of fashion photography almost everywhere we look on TV, newspapers, internet and all media. Dazzling women with long legs and tanned skin scream for attention on news stands all over the place. It is the fashion photographer who is primarily responsible to bring those photographers to us, the everyday people. Unlike what one often imagines, there is more to fashion photography than a glitzy life style, fun and happening models. In fact there is a lot of planning involved behind every single fashion photograph that we see.

A name such as Mario Testino has become iconic in the realm of fashion photography. Did you know that photographers like him are just as sought after as the models that they photograph? At times the photographer is an even bigger celebrity than the model.

This profession may seem dream like to the young and enthusiastic photographer but it is not all about fun and glitz. It is not just about meeting the rich and the famous, the fat checks and the feeling of rock that goes with fashion photography. Did you know, for every one photographer that is successful, there are hundreds who are left looking for shoots for many years? Many give up after a few years while some do go on to become successful later on in life.

If you want to become a fashion photographer

1. Learn the art well

There is no end to learning. Here is where many a youngster goes astray. they are so bothered about the style and the glamour associated with the fashion photographer, they concentrate more on looking right than shooting right. Know your photography so well that it comes naturally to you. Get books on the subject and read them to expand your knowledge of the subject.

2. Equipment

Next to the right knowledge comes the right equipment. Here is a hard truth - you cannot be a good fashion photographer unless you can afford expensive equipment. Cameras are not cheap, and you have new ones coming out every season. If you cannot afford to start off with a good camera and lighting system, your knowledge would go to waste.

Digital Photography Inside Out!

3. The portfolio

The portfolio of a photographer is what finally lands the job. Make sure you have an impressive folio with your best work carefully selected. Choose the best 4 by 5 slide images you have. Some prefer to make prints. It is suggested - if you are discussing something with a photography pro, carry the slides. If it is a designer you are meeting the prints may be a better idea and more convenient for everyone.

4. Personality

Any editor is looking for original talent, so make sure you have a strong individual point of view. It is ok to be affected by another professional's point of view, as long as you add or remove from it to make it unique and different. You need an identity!

Digital Photography Inside Out!

Food Photography Tips for Newbie's

When you see an image of a tasty dish in a magazine you wish you had shot your self - keep in mind that a lot of planning must have gone behind that shot. If you wish to shoot similar images you too could get started with this article,

Lighting

You cannot have a good photograph without the right lighting. Do try and visit the place you are going to be shooting beforehand. Have a look at the lighting and remember that ambient light can be enough in most kitchens, since they are very neatly lit up. On the other hand if you prefer to have a little more control over the lighting you could carry one flash and even a few slaves for high lights. Also, you may have yellowish hues when you are shooting under bulb lights (ambient). If you want this then leave it just like that. Alternatively, a high shutter speed and flash would remove the yellow haze, and you could work on it on Photoshop as well. Just use the color balance option to decrease the yellow there.

Tripod

If you are shooting under ambient light then you may need to use a slow shutter speed. This makes it inevitable to use a tripod. Get the sturdiest tripod you can afford to carry to the venue. And then you will probably be shooting close ups of the food. Here again the importance of a tripod becomes more than necessary.

The Food arrangement

Where you are photographing food, presentation is everything. Take the time to symmetrically arrange the food items, and the cutlery around it. Make sure you let the best thing about the food stand out. For example, if its chocolate pudding you are photographing, let the chocolate sauce flow well over the pudding to give it that special feel that makes you taste chocolate just by looking at the image. It were a burger, you would want to make sure the ham is stuffing out of the sides of the bun.

Digital Photography Inside Out!

Depth of Field

Professional food photos almost always have a shallow depth of field. In fact if you are using a professional view camera you could get everything out of focus except for a few inches in the area the food is kept in. Out of focus table cloths and chairs are classic food backgrounds. Auto model cameras will not allow you to adjust this, but you could get the effect on computer later. However it is much better to shoot so as to get that shallow depth of field - a computer cannot get quite the same effect.

Finally remember, the food doesn't have to taste good when you are shooting - it only has to look good. Professional photographers sometimes go as far as to blow torch certain areas of a barbecued chicken to make it look better!

Digital Photography Inside Out!

Proper Makeup As A Technique In Photography

A fashion photographer photographs models of all age groups, day in and day out. Did you know, it is not just photography that makes a good fashion photograph? Make up, and the elegance of the model of course, are equally important in a fashion photo shoot, if not more. When any of these elements of photography, model quality and make up quality are substandard, the resulting image would be a substandard image. The photographer needs to concern himself with elements such as the lenses and the cameras used, the background, the composition and the lighting. Those are his areas of expertise. The model needs to show up fresh and radiant for the shoot. Finally the make up artist has to work towards covering up the model's bad negative qualities and enhancing his or her positive features.

A few make up tips

Make up does have a big effect on the quality of the photo shoot. The very beauty products which we see in ads and on the market stores could be used in the studio to make a better picture. Normally the make up artist would have a few assistants that each specialize in a certain area of make up.

Concealer

Any hu7man being has a few dark spots around the face area, and these can easily be hidden with a little bit of concealer, as the name suggests it conceals the spots giving the skin an overall symmetry.

Foundation

Foundation is applied on all areas of the face, and sometimes on hands and legs as well (just for the shoots - this is not mandatory make up). The foundation gives an overall smoothness to the skin, making it appear uniform in shade and tan.

Powder

Powder can be applied to the forehead and the cheeks to light the area up under the flash. Powder is generally a part of any lady's make up box, and it does not take much skill in applying.

Digital Photography Inside Out!

Eyebrows

Make up men can bring a fresh feel to the face by working on the eyebrows. Eye pencils can be used around the eyes to give the model's gaze a harder and intimate feel. Eye shadow is applied keeping the mood of the shoot and the color of the model's clothes in mind. It is generally applied in limited quantities. Eye liner could be used to remove the look of fatigue, if the model does have that after many hours of shooting.

Lipstick

This is generally the final make up touch that is applied, and the make up specialists usually use lip gloss and pencil to add the finishing to the lipstick.

Make up is something that need not take a lot of time. It can be done in only a few minutes, but it is not something that can be perfected in a day. The right man/woman can do a great job in a few minutes only, while the photographer changes his lighting for example.

Tips on Capturing Moments in Travel

As we all know, traveling is a fun past time. You may visit places that you will get to see only once in your life. Why not capture the memory on photographs? For photo enthusiasts, getting the images is just as important as the idea of reaching a destination.

Some tips on how you can get better travel images

1. Carry the right gear

If you are looking to buy new gear before your next travel plan, you will need to make a basic choice between a compact camera and a Single Lens Reflex variety. It is unfair to say one is better than the other. It is a matter of how skilled you are to use the SLR, since it is a complex machine. When you use the SLR variety, you do have the added advantage of interchangeable lenses and zillions of gadgets to go with it. You could choose to buy ultra wide lenses for interiors and long focal length tele lenses for wild life images. On the other hand, these cameras are heavy to hold, difficult to master and more expensive. A compact will probably have a good range zoom inbuilt and will be much easier to use if photography is not something you wish to take the time to learn.

Digital Photography Inside Out!

2. The right film

If you are among those who still prefer film over digital, that is fine - many people do. Well, you need to choose film as per the call of the hour. Generally speaking you will want fast film, or film with a high ISO rating like 400 or 800, if you are shooting in low light or with long lenses. If the light is adequate you will want slower film, such as 100 or 200 - they provide better quality. Make sure you carry enough film and batteries not to be left without any means to shoot at an awkward time. Keep exposed film in a separate bag or compartment so it doesn't get mixed up with new batches of film.

3. Get adequate information about where you are headed

As mentioned in the previous paragraph, you will need to plan ahead for the trip. Some situations of extremely cold or hot climate may require special clothing for you and protection for your camera. Use an underwater camera housing even if you just plan to shoot on the beach. The sand and spray can ruin a camera and its lens, especially where modern lenses with minute motors built in are concerned.

4. Maintain a journal

Do not ever leave your viewers left wondering what an image means. Every picture should be a story in itself. Note the data, time, place and exposure of the images where possible, so you can relate incidents as you show your images to family and friends.

Digital Photography Inside Out!

How To Capture Those Perfect Wedding Moments

A wedding is one of the most important events in a couple's life. Storing its memories in the form of photographs is right on the top of the list of plans for the wedding. Wedding photography is something that has evolved into a few categories over the years. You need to understand and give a name to what you want from your photography.

1. Choosing the right guy for the job

When you see an image of a wedding album that you love, ask your self why you liked it. Portrait photographers tend to make people pose before they shoot, and will often bring in lighting with them. You would get good poses, and no awkward moments. It is always better to work with a professional rather than with a friend who is a photo enthusiast, so it is a bad idea to try and save money on the photographer. Of late, it has become popular to use a photojournalist for the job. Photojournalists never pose people and tend to shoot candid images which are a true representation of the mood that was ambient at the wedding. This is currently the hot favorite with couples getting married.

2. The Right Gear

A wedding photographer would typically get a digital SLR camera or else a medium format squarish camera for the job. He may bring a few lights which would need to be set up before the ceremonies begin. There are still some photographers who prefer to use film. This is more or less his business, and it is not good to try and control what the photographers use. But here is a tip - professionals generally do not use compact cameras other than for scouting purposes. If you feel that the photographer does not have adequate equipment, there is no harm in discussing this with the person.

3. The Black and White Option

Black and White has suddenly re-emerged as a favorite medium for wedding photography. It is normally the photographer who decides which images would be printed in black and white and which in color, but you can definitely request a few particular ones in monotone. Usually the professionals of today prefer to shoot everything in digital color, and later change selected images to black and white.

4. Personality

The personality of any photographer is reflected in his or her work. Do hold an informal interview with the photographer - you do not want a person who seems antisocial and reserved. You would want an outgoing person with a pleasing personality for your wedding photography. On the other hand, you wouldn't want someone who is interfering and self centered as well. Some photographers insist on ruining the best moments by interfering with ceremonies and speeches. So try and get the person with the right personality, which would be a balance of both extremes mentioned here.

Digital Photography Inside Out!

The Use Of Filters In Photography

In this modern age, people think of filters only as options on Adobe Photoshop. Many forget that filters were and still are glass rings that are screwed on to the front of your lens, to provide the special effects. It is true however that Photoshop can mimic the same on computer, so many photographers choose NOT to use the glass filters, and later edit the photographs on computer. It is good though, to have an idea of what filters really are, even if you are a great Photoshop user.

1. Blur filters

Say you were shooting a waterfall at the bottom, where you can see the spray from the water form a cloudy area. The camera may capture it as separate droplets of sharp water, and you may NOT want that effect. You could however get the cloudy effect by adding a blur filter in front of your lens. You can get the same effect by using the blur filter of diffuse filter in Adobe Photoshop. Some do it this way; some prefer to do it that way.

2. UV filter

Did you know that ultra violet light from the sun can affect your film? You could use a good ultra violet filter on your lens to remove any UV entering your camera. Since they are clear filters you can leave one of these on every lens. Not only does this serve the purpose of keeping the UV out, you protect the expensive lens coating when you constantly have a UV filter attached on top. Photoshop can't do that for you!

3. Star filter

Have you seen record labels from the 70s with the disco lights looking like stars? Well that is the effect you can get with a star filter. A star filter makes any point light (like a bulb but not a tube light) appear as if there were rays coming out and making it twinkle like a star does. This filter is very useful when you want to add the feeling of glamour in a setting. Say for example a fashion show?

4. D.O.F. filters

There are filters that can give a shallow depth of field effect even on a small aperture (which is supposed to five long depth of field). They are the fog and the mist filters, which have a clear center in the glass filter, but diffused all around. You may have seen images where the center of the image where to model is located, is sharp and it is blurred everywhere else. This is how they get that effect - the mist and fog filters.

5. Color Correction Filters

You can use color correction filters to enhance or reduce certain colors. When you have studied complimentary colors you have the power o use complimentary filters when you want a lesser shade of a certain hue. On the other hand, you could enhance a certain shade by using the same color filter.

Digital Photography Inside Out!

Filters For Special Effects

Maybe you have seen photographs in magazines and on the net that look surrealistic or unreal. Most of them have no doubt been edited on computer, but some have been affected during the shooting process. This can be achieved with the use of glass rings called filters. They fit on to the front of your lens. Filters are available in a variety of categories and effects, and let us discuss some of them.

Black and white filters

Black and white filters are in fact made of colored glass! Their importance could be hard to understand by a person who has no clue about black and white photography. It is out of the scope of this article to explain why color filters affect black and white film, but we shall explain the effect. If you shoot a blue sky using a red filter, the sky appears darkish. this is because blue and red are complimentary colors like black and white. The red filter allows all other colors to pass through it, except for blue. And so, the image remains unaffected except for the blue areas which come out blackish. This is in fact the beauty of black and white photography, and it can never be faked or cloned on computers and digital cameras.

Color Filters

Color filters or filters for general use come in a variety of categories. The multi image filter multiplies the center of the image so you see many images repeated, like the disco effect of the seventies. The star filters make a point of light to appear as a star. They are very good for commercial uses. Have you ever seen images in magazines that make the model's skin glow as if there was a soft light around the face alone? Well that effect is achieved with the diffusing filter. It softens the light as well as removes the blemishes of the skin. Never use this if sharpness is your main objective, such as when shooting interiors. It is good for portraits though. And then there is the warm tone filter which adds a warm effect to the skin. Other filters such as red and orange can add a dramatic effect to a sunset. Have you seen images where the center of the photo is clear but everything else is out of focus? That is done with the center spot filter, which has clear glass in the center of the filter alone, but diffuses all around it. These are just a few of the filters that one can use to get some amazing effects on photographs. Many if not all of the color effects can be done on computer today, so we now see a rise in shooting

Digital Photography Inside Out!

basic raw, sharp images which are later enhanced on computer using software such as the popular Adobe Photoshop.

Digital Photography Inside Out!

Focus And Get The Best Out Of A Shot

Indoor Photography

When shooting indoors you could use a high speed film setting such as ISO 400 or 800. This makes the camera more sensitive to light and thereby you can get a decent exposure even in low light conditions. With modern digital cameras, you can immediately see a preview of the shot and decide if the light was adequate. If your camera has an auto focus option you should use it to focus accurately on your subject. Where light is too low for this feature, some models have a built in focusing light (such as the Fuji fine professional series). In the absence of this feature it is better to focus manually if light is too low for the auto focus.

When the light is just not enough, the camera compensates for this by letting the light enter for more time, and this is done by leaving your shutter open for maybe a second or more duration. If handheld, your pictures would have an undesirable shake effect in such case. Correct this be either turning on the flash indoors, or if it is still life you are photographing, using a tripod would do the trick.

Power

When shooting indoors, it generally requires more power, whether using the flash or using tripod as may be the case. If you have a lot of low light photography planned, remember this means you run the risk of running out of battery sooner than normal. Auto focus can be very badly affected by low battery power, and this pretty much takes the joy out of your photography.

Glare

Have you ever had images with certain areas too bright? This happens when a source of light is directly in front of you, and also by reflections off the flash. The flash light can reflect a glare off something like a mirror in the room. You could correct this by shooting from a different angle.

Composition

Composition is how you frame the shot. Keep a balance in your photography frames, and work towards not cutting off parts of people's faces. And do try and concentrate on the background as

Digital Photography Inside Out!

well. For example a lamp post right behind the subject's head is an undesirable element in the photo. Also, make sure you are not obstructing any part of the lens with woolens etc.

Outdoor

Outdoor photography can be done with film speeds as low as ISO 50, and sometimes even less. The low film speed means the camera becomes less sensitive to light but it also increases the sharpness and quality of the grain. If you are photographing people who need to squint because of the sun, do reposition the subjects if possible. You could get the sun on the side rather than right behind you. But never in front of the camera or that would cause a glare effect.

Digital Photography Inside Out!

Use A Telephoto Lens For Your Aquarium

Having an aquarium is a wonderful past time, and if you are passionate about photography as well as aquarium fish, you may want to make some nice images of your fish. As with any kind of photography, the two most important elements remain lighting and composition.

Lighting the Aquarium

Try and light the aquarium from the top. You could add reflectors on the outside and under the aquarium to get a variety of results. For example if you would like to accentuate the aqua feel, add a blue reflector right opposite the light source, in this case that would be under the aquarium. You could also use a blue gel on the light source to create blue light. Before you begin shooting, give the fish adequate time to get used to the gear suddenly appearing around the sides of their aquarium world, Fish are more aware of their surroundings than you may imagine. If you do not want to see your fish jumping out of the aquarium in terror, work slowly and calmly, and do not make sudden movements. Give them time to get used to any new feature you want to add. For example, if you've just placed the flash light looking down on the aquarium; give it a few minutes before you add a reflector.

Composition

Getting your aquarium fish into focus as they dart around the container is not very easy, especially if you wish to shoot close ups. For close up shots you may need to use extension rings and tubes between the camera and the lens. Take a few minutes to get used to the sideways motion of the fish before you begin shooting. If the fish are moving sideways, you can minimize the depth of field since they are more or less equally far from the lens when moving from this end to that. You could even fix the camera on a tripod for a smooth left-right-left motion. As you pan the tripod, fire the shutter while still in the slow movement. This can create some exciting effects, and minimize the blur on the fish. If the fish are moving towards you on the other hand, you would want to quickly change to maximum possible depth of field, since the distance between you and them is on the decrease.

Digital Photography Inside Out!

Exposure

You will not have time to calculate exposure every time you change the depth of filed. It is a good idea to set the camera on aperture priority mode if you have the feature, and let the camera worry about the changes in shutter speed as you change the aperture.

Safety

When working with lighting equipment, make absolutely sure that the flash head is secure on the stand. If it comes off the stand and falls into the aquarium, the electricity would immediately kill the fish.

Digital Photography Inside Out!

Techniques For Underwater Photography

Underwater photography is something fascinating that has been enabled by technology in the not so distant past. In the years gone by, it was only the divers who ever got to actually see the underwater world. However thanks to underwater photographers, we are now able to get a glimpse of the deep seas right from the comfort of our homes - through television and in print media, also on the internet. It is true that any form of photography requires a certain amount of skill. Underwater photography on the other hand needs one to be a proficient diver as well as a good photographer.

As far as general wild life photography is concerned, photographers can work from a distance and photograph their subjects. But where underwater photography needs to be done, they need to get up close to the subject. This is simply because water refracts or bends light rays. Observe this phenomenon by putting your hand into a bucket of water. The closer you bring it to the surface of water the clearer it appears to be. So, the less the light needs to travel through the water, the less is the distortion. This is why underwater photographers have to get as close to their subjects as possible.

In the underwater world, it is not as simple a philosophy as survival of the fittest through speed. Most fish choose camouflage as the solution to predators. This is why you need to be skilled at spotting your fish when you are an underwater photographer. So, this is an added quality that you need to have to shoot underwater photographs successfully. Not only do you need to be a good diver, and a good photographer but also a good marine biologists. Where this is not always possible, photographers dive alongside biologists to get the best pictures. And then, some marine animals die if you as much as touch them, so it requires a certain amount of knowledge in any case, to dive responsibly.

The gear

You could get a housing for your regular camera to shoot underwater. This is nothing but a plastic, water tight container for your camera that allows all of the functions to still be accessible from the outside. Or else, you could use underwater cameras specially designed for the purpose. Photographers who shoot only underwater photography prefer to use underwater cameras, while those who shoot underwater only at times may use the underwater housing with their regular cameras. You can also attach an underwater strobe flash unit where you are

Digital Photography Inside Out!

shooting deep into the ocean. On the shallow areas, sunlight is enough to light the underwater world.

Underwater photographers tend to try and shoot their subjects from under them, since they hide into the backgrounds. Also, the sunlight from top can create interesting background hues.

Digital Photography Inside Out!

Forensic Photography Used In Today's Society

Have you seen television images on crime scenes where the yellow tape has concealed an area and police officials are walking around busily behind it? It is just there that we see the guy with the camera bag and lighting walking around taking photographs of the scene of the crime. Although police try their best to get every bit of evidence from the scene of the crime, the photographs can play a vital role when the crime scene needs to be discussed or imagined later. They also prove as a great record to go with the files in the state department or sheriff's office. Photographs are of course a vital part of every investigation that takes place today, and they hold as valid evidence in the court of law.

There is no better tool to catalog the data of a scene of crime than the camera. The camera helps preserve the scene of the crime as it really was. Many a time when something is overlooked during investigation, the detective in charge refers to these images to look for clues, as that is all they have at a later date when the crime scene has been disturbed.

An eye for detail is the most important quality that a forensic photographer must have. There is no compromise on sharpness in any form of photography, but it is absolutely vital where forensics is concerned. There could be a small piece of glass in a shadow area for example that the detectives didn't notice. But they will, later when they see the enlarged view of the photographs of the crime scene, over a cup of coffee at the station. Nothing more needs to be said about why sharpness is critical here.

The forensic photographer is allowed to take the photographs at the scene of the crime before any of the other officials get to touch the place. The idea is the preserve the crime scene as close to how it was at the moment the crime occurred. Once he is done taking his pictures, the fingerprints are brushed and the murder weapon if any is removed, the body is removed and the investigation for other clues begins. But nothing is allowed to be touched until the photographer has completed his or her job. But they do continue to take photographs during the investigative procedures as well.

The forensic photographers are instructed to get a long range, mid range and an ultra close up of every angle. Using the wrong lens or the wrong angle can mislead the viewer to judge the wrong distance between the elements of the photograph. The forensic photographer also takes

Digital Photography Inside Out!

notes of every photo that is taken. A lot of thought goes behind the angle, the lighting and the lens - so as to give an image as close to reality as possible - nothing more and nothing less.

Digital Photography Inside Out!

Digital Stock Photography's Ability to Sell for You

Digital stock photography makes up for a large portion of the images that you see all around you on a daily basis. Commercials, mailers, and magazines are all full of digital stock photography that perfectly communicates the picture takers message. A blooming rose does in fact help sell face cream as well as anything else that is meant to regenerate. stock photography is a smart way to make an idea stand out just a little bit more.

The Power of Digital Stock Photography

The impact that visual imagery has to offer has been a subject of interest to marketing gurus for years. No one can exactly pinpoint why the average human being is so stimulated and influenced by images and pictures, but the effects cannot be denied. Think about it, Florida beach photos conjure feelings of relaxation just as a photo of a smiling little girl implies and even creates a happy and nostalgic feeling of fulfillment.

If your goal is to use digital stock photography as a means to sell an idea or product, digital stock photography can be your greatest tool. Your message is reinforced by the visual aura of the presentation when this is the means of doing it. Business stock photos are one way to establish a professional image in the public mind before you even open your mouth. Digital stock photography can also help to make or break your reputation by conveying your character traits and ideals.

It has been said a million times that a picture is worth a thousand words. This is especially the case with digital stock photography. The spatial real estate that a yellow pages ad or business card offers you is not all that much. You need to make the highest impact in a very tiny space. The best stock images can help you do just that by representing you and what you stand for in just one quick look.

If you use digital stock photography to sell or advertise your products and services, you are guaranteeing your customers a solid glimpse into what they can expect from you. It is a great idea for anyone. You can use this also a means of advertising a special event such as a family

Digital Photography Inside Out!

reunion or anything else too. Nothing will get the imagination of most people in the same way as a great photo will.

If you prefer to learn all the basics yourself you can always go into a digital photography class for help. If you really want to be able to take excellent digital photographs, you can certainly find everything that you need including the camera and the software online or at your local retailers. Digital cameras are so popular these days you can find them just about anywhere. You just want to find a camera that will do what you want it to. You want a camera that offers great pictures as well as easy docking options for downloading to your printer or computer.

Digital Photography Inside Out!

Should You Go to Photography School?

Photography is tough business. You need to know the ropes of business and not just the artistic aspect of photography, if you are to make it on your own as a professional photographer. And then you need to be good enough at your skill to realize what lens is right for what particular conditions. Being a hobbyist photographer is a whole different thing, and being a professional is quite another. If you are really serious about taking this up as a means to earn your livelihood, why not consider going to photography school?

It is true that you can become a good photographer without a degree, as many have in the past. However a few classes are only going to help you along the way. If you are completely new to the subject you should at least get a basic course. You will find a variety of courses out there, and things like continuing education and distance education are great ways to learn the subject without giving it 100% of your time. More often than not, short courses are enough to get one hooked on to the craft and therefore take a few more complicated courses and workshops.

Distance Learning

If you have a job then distance learning can really be it for you. You could continue with your current schedule and never take a risk. If you learn enough and are confident with a few assignments under your belt, then you can leave the day job and concentrate full time on your shooting.

The various choices in photography

Photography is a general term used to describe a variety of professionals. You could be an underwater photographer, an aerial photographer or a fashion photographer just to name a few. As you can well imagine, the only similarity between the three classes mentioned above is the use of the camera. An underwater photographer would need additional training in diving, an aerial photographer would need to be trained in the safety of the skies and a fashion photographer needs to have an eye for fashion. You need to ask yourself what branch of photography you are best cut out for, and take your time to decide on this before you begin building a portfolio around the topic. This is where a training in the subject can really assist you to evaluate your self. When you are given assignments in school to shoot this or that, you

Digital Photography Inside Out!

quickly begin to understand what you are cut out for. If you are not a very social person, fashion and weddings is not for you, but you may be excellent at real estate photography.

The diversity you find in courses

When you take a course you are opened up to various kinds of photography. Assignments which you work with for your grades could range from fashion, to still life, to high speed photography. This exposure is crucial as you decide on your future job prospects.

Digital Photography Inside Out!

Schools That Teach Photography

It simply isn't true that you will have to go to years of bachelor school to become a photographer. You could simply choose photography as an ancillary subject to whatever it is that you may already be studying. You may be wondering if you could learn the subject without attending the classes at all, and the answer to this one is YES. If you have the dedication to try out new ideas and the equipment to see them through you can definitely train your own self to be a photographer.

And then there is the option of distance education that most photographers love simply because it gives them the freedom to experiment on their own while still getting a recognized degree at the end of the day. The NY Institute of photography is a fine example of a college offering such an option.

You will need to get educated on elements of photography such as lighting, exposure, composition and lenses. Of course you can take this course even while you are working at a job, since it is a distance education thing. Any photography course should also include a good amount of practical shooting exposure. Generally about half the emphasis goes on the portfolio that you can make by the end of every assignment.

You don't need chemicals any more!

Gone are the days when a photographer had to learn dark room techniques to develop and correct his or her own work. Today with digital photography all you need is a personal computer to edit your images. Keep in mind though that learning a software to edit your images is not as easy as it sounds. While it is a matter of minutes before you learn how to handle brightness, contrast and exposure level on a computer it is much more challenging to make major changes to a photograph, and that is something that will probably not be a part of your photography course. Adobe Photoshop is a favorite photo editing software among photographers.

Of course, getting into photography school full time could be the best option if you have the time. But there have been many successful photographers who never went to school at all. All that counts when you meet a client is the quality of your sample photo album, what photographers call their portfolio. Get this right and you have a chance. Luckily photography is not yet a field where employers have begun asking for degrees. Still, if you wish to get into

Digital Photography Inside Out!

something as complex and as challenging as medical photography, neither can you learn it on your own and nor can you hope to get a job without a qualification.

There are many ways to become a photographer, and getting a degree in photography is one of the ways. Don't let the lack of college education ever stop you from chasing your dreams.

Digital Photography Inside Out!

How To Start A Photography Business

So you wish to start a photography business? Well that is not as difficult as some people make it out to be. You could start your photography service right from your own home, with almost no expense at all, if you already own the gear. And we believe anyone considering starting their own photography business will probably already own a good flash and camera.

The right approach

It is easy to say that you are going to start shooting commercially, but it takes a bit of experience to be as dedicated as a commercial photographer. Even if you are an advanced photographer, and have never charged for a photograph all your life, you have a couple of things to learn still. Remember, when you are charging a client a fee there is no excuse for a bad photograph. We do not mean to judge your capability as a photographer. All we are trying to say is there may be situations where you will go ahead and shoot outdoors in low light if you are shooting for free, but you should think twice about such situations where you are charging a fee. One bad image and people will start calling you a bad photographer. It is therefore much safer for you to be a little fussy and do not shoot at all unless you know you will get the perfect lighting and composition. That is the mark of a professional, and only time will tell you when you have reached that point. When you are shooting for your own self you try and make do with what you have available. When you are shooting for money, you do not settle for anything other than the best situation.

The Miscellaneous expenses

When you do begin a photo business, you will need to print stationary and business cards. A website is a great idea to promote your service, as is leaflets and brochures. Since you probably already have the major expense of equipment taken care of like we assume, these should not pose a big threat to your wallet. Take the time to design all areas of your business and the 'office' if at home or outside. If you have a basement area you can convert into a studio there's nothing like it. Build your collection of accessories when you can. Get a slave light now and a back ground cloth then. This is a cost effective way into the business. The approach would be totally different when you want to open a commercial photo studio where your livelihood depends on it. What we have put down is a plan for you to ease your self into the market while you still have your day job. If all goes well, and you have a few regular clients, then go ahead

Digital Photography Inside Out!

and take the plunge by dedicating all your time to the new venture. All the best!

Digital Photography Inside Out!

This Product Is Brought To You By

DAVID A OSEI

www.ingramcontent.com/pod-product-compliance
Lightning Source LLC
Chambersburg PA
CBHW030521220526
45463CB00007B/2670